YOUR WORLD

YOUR FRIENDS

Michael Pollard

Photographs by Tim Woodcock

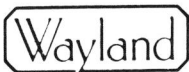

Wayland

Your World

Your Community
Your Family
Your Friends
Yourself

First published in 1989 by
Wayland (Publishers) Limited
61, Western Road, Hove
East Sussex, BN3 1JD, England

© Copyright 1989 Wayland (Publishers) Limited

Series Editor: Mike Hirst
Series Designer: Sally Boothroyd

British Library Cataloguing in Publication Data
Pollard, Michael, *1931–*
    Your friends.
    1. Children. Friendship
    I. Title II. Series
    305.2'3

ISBN 1 85210 761 8

Typeset by L. George & R. Gibbs, Wayland
Printed and bound by Casterman, S.A., Belgium.

Contents

All the words that appear in
bold are explained in the
glossary on page 22.

Friends are people who like one another.

Your friends are people you like to play with and talk to. They may live near you or go to the same school as you.

We can have fun with our friends.

Our friends are the people we like best.

You choose your friends because you like being with them and they like being with you. When you are with your friends you feel safe and happy together.

You can share with your friends.

Friends like to share things between them. Good friends share their sweets and toys. Sometimes they give presents to each other.

Sharing your sweets is one way of being friendly.

Friends like to help each other too. If you have something difficult to do, you can ask a friend to help you.

Friends can help us to learn new things

Friends like doing things together.

Friends enjoy doing the same kind of things. They like to spend a lot of time together.

These friends are playing hopscotch.

Friends like playing the same
games and watching the same
programmes on television.
Sometimes they visit each other
after school or at **weekends**. At
school, friends often like doing
work together.

*It is fun to play
a computer
game with a
friend.*

Good friends talk to each other.

It is important to spend time talking to our friends. We can tell them what makes us happy. We can talk to them if we are sad or in trouble.

We can tell our friends about our feelings.

Friends like to talk and joke with each other.

Sometimes we tell them **secrets**. Things seem less **worrying** if you talk to your friends about them.

It is good fun to have a day out with your friends.

Friends often go out together, on a **picnic** or a visit to the **funfair**. When you have had a day out with your friends, you can all talk about it afterwards and remember what a good time you had.

Do you enjoy a picnic with your friends?

Everyone looks forward to a day out.

A happy day out with your friends is something you may remember for a long time.

When you are away from your friends you can write to them or ring them up.

Our friends like to hear from us when we are away. Friends send each other **postcards** when they are on holiday.

We can write to our friends when we are on holiday.

14

We can use the phone to keep in touch with our friends.

Sometimes friends write long letters or talk on the phone. We like to be reminded of our friends, and we like to tell our friends how we are getting on.

Even friends sometimes quarrel, but they soon make it up.

Sometimes even the best of friends do not agree.

No one agrees with their friends all the time.

But when their **quarrel** is over they soon forget all about it and are good friends again. They show that they are sorry for being **angry**, and make up their quarrel by being especially kind.

We can still be friends when we have stopped arguing.

Making new friends can be difficult.

If you move house or go to a new school, you might feel shy.

When you are at a new school, you sometimes feel lonely.

It is hard to talk to people you don't know and make new friends. But new friends are interesting. There is a lot to find out about them. If a new person comes to your school, you can get to know them. Then they will not feel lonely.

You stop feeling lonely when you make new friends.

Some people stay friends all their lives.

Even if they move away, friends may go on writing to each other and see each other from time to time. Perhaps your mother or father still have friends they made when they were children.

Photos remind us of our old friends.

There is a lot to talk about when you meet old friends again.

Sometimes old friends take their holidays together or go to visit each other.

Glossary

Angry   Cross.

Funfair   A place with stalls and rides where you go to have a good time.

Picnic   A meal that you eat out of doors.

Postcard   A card that you send through the post. It often has a picture on one side.

Quarrel   An argument.

Secrets   Things that you don't tell everyone.

Weekends   Saturdays and Sundays.

Worrying   Making you unhappy.

Books to read

Health and Friends   Dorothy Baldwin
   (Wayland, 1987).
Health and Feelings   Dorothy Baldwin
   (Wayland, 1987).
The World of Play   Anna Sproule
   (Macdonald, 1988).
Five Stones and Knuckle Bones   Chris Deshpande
   (A. and C. Black, 1988).

Picture acknowledgements

Topham Picture Library 19; Jennie Woodcock 4, 7, 8; Tim Woodcock *cover*, 6, 9, 10, 11, 12, 14, 15, 16, 17, 18, 20, 21; ZEFA 5, 13.

Index